WITHDRAWN

The Drive of Your Life

The Drive of Your Life

Lisa de Silva

Illustrations by Sheri Gee

HAY HOUSE

HAY HOUSE
Australia • Canada • Hong Kong
South Africa • United Kingdom • United States

Published and distributed in the United Kingdom by Hay House UK Ltd, Unit 62, Canalot Studios, 222 Kensal Rd, London W10 5BN. Tel.: (44) 20 8962 1230; Fax: (44) 20 8962 1239. www.hayhouse.co.uk

Published and distributed in the United States of America by Hay House, Inc., PO Box 5100, Carlsbad, CA 92018-5100. Tel.: (1) 760 431 7695 or (800) 654 5126; Fax: (1) 760 431 6948 or (800) 650 5115. www.hayhouse.com

Published and distributed in Australia by Hay House Australia Ltd, 18/36 Ralph St, Alexandria NSW 2015. Tel.: (61) 2 9669 4299; Fax: (61) 2 9669 4144. www.hayhouse.com.au

Published and distributed in the Republic of South Africa by Hay House SA (Pty), Ltd, PO Box 990, Witkoppen 2068. Tel./Fax: (27) 11 706 6612. orders@psdprom.co.za

Distributed in Canada by Raincoast, 9050 Shaughnessy St, Vancouver, BC V6P 6E5. Tel.: (1) 604 323 7100; Fax: (1) 604 323 2600.

© Lisa de Silva, 2005

Design: Leanne Siu • *Illustrations* © Sheri Gee, 2005

The author of this book does not dispense medical advice or prescribe the use of any technique as a form of treatment for physical or medical problems without the advice of a physician, either directly or indirectly. The intent of the author is only to offer information of a general nature to help you in your quest for emotional and spiritual well-being. In the event you use any of the information in this book for yourself, which is your constitutional right, the author and the publisher assume no responsibility for your actions.

A catalogue record for this book is available from the British Library.

ISBN 1-4019-0693-1

Printed and bound in Great Britain by. TJ International, Padstow, Cornwall.

For My Family and Friends

Past and Present

Contents

Are You on the Path to Joy and Contentment or Just Driving Yourself Crazy?

Imagine you've been handed the keys to a brand new car — it is the perfect model, size and colour for you. You feel excited and grateful, and you're looking forward to all the wonderful adventures, interesting places and people you will meet on your travels. You open the door, climb in, position the seat and mirror so they're exactly right for you. Then, with excitement bubbling in your tummy, you turn on the engine and head off.

Feeling happy and confident that you can travel anywhere you please, you start getting used to the controls, the way the steering responds, the power of the engine — when suddenly you realise that you are not alone!

No. In fact, your car is stuffed full of passengers – there are your parents, your brothers, sisters, partner, children, friends, colleagues, people you don't even know. And they are all shouting at you:

Take a left here!

Slow down!

Change up now!

You don't want to go that way, there'll be traffic!

Mind the kerb!

Careful, you nearly hit that car!

Can you drop me over there?

No – take the third exit, not the fourth!

Oh dear! After a while you may forget wherever it was you wanted to go or give up trying to get there altogether. For you, driving is fast becoming a source of stress not joy. You may be questioning your ability to drive, or you may even avoid venturing out at all.

So, how do you cope? Do you:

Resign yourself to becoming a chauffeur?

Become a passenger and let someone else do the driving?

Put the car back in the garage and don't go out at all?

Avoid driving as much as possible by distracting yourself with minor repair jobs and worries about fuel consumption?

Shut out everything and everyone in order to focus on your destination, only to feel disappointed and dissatisfied when you eventually arrive there?

At times driving can be scary, aimless or just not particularly enjoyable. You will get stuck in traffic or become lost, run out of fuel or even break down. But this little book is here to help you cope with those situations, and learn to experience more of the sheer pleasure that driving can offer.

If you're reading *The Drive of Your Life* you're probably not totally happy with your current journey. Maybe:

You're not enjoying it as much as you could be.

You feel lost.

You feel you're going in the wrong direction.

You've arrived at your chosen destination, but feel disappointed – you sense that something is still missing.

Yet fear not – help is at hand. This book has been written as a manual, a sort of Highway Code to help you navigate your path. *The Drive of Your Life* is not about changing you or improving you. It's about exploring and understanding your unique spirit, and what you as an individual need in order to get the maximum pleasure, enjoyment and satisfaction from your journey.

Getting Ready To Go

1

1
Getting Ready to Go

The Drive of Your Life is intended to be fun, with a series of practical activities designed to be enjoyed. Because some sections will be more appropriate for you than others, according to how your journey is progressing, it has been structured like a reference book, allowing you to refer back to it as it suits you.

All you need is a notebook, a pen, and the willingness to commit some time. A word of warning here: if, as you flick through the rest of this book, you decide that you are too busy, tired or hungry to do the activities involved, this may provide a clue as to why your journey isn't currently as good as it could be!

Activity 1

Creating a Log Book

Your first task is to create a log book for you and your journey.

- 🙂 Find or buy a notebook and pen that are attractive to you and which you will enjoy using.

- 🙂 You may wish to customise your notebook. Be as creative as you like – sew a jacket for it, or knit, paint or draw one. Cover it with beautiful paper, stick pictures, photographs or words you love on it – just do whatever makes the notebook attractive to you.

- 🙂 If none of the above appeals, simply take pleasure from shopping for a notebook that you'll enjoy using.

3

Driving In The Right Spirit

2

2
Driving in the Right Spirit

The Drive of Your Life is about you finding and learning to trust *your* spirit, *your* intuition, *your* heart, *your* inner guide. Call it what you will, it's that subconscious part of you that *knows* what's right for you as an individual. This book is about learning to listen to it.

We all have our own interpretation or word for this part of us. Here's a selection:

> *Spirit/heart/soul*

> *Intuition/gut instinct/subconscious*

Inner guide/angel/god

Passion/creativity

Joy/lightness/laughter

Love/compassion/kindness

In the body/mind/spirit equation, much time, money and effort have gone into helping us understand the workings of our bodies and minds. *The Drive of Your Life* is about finding and connecting to your spiritual side. Ignoring this side of you will leave you with a sense of something missing, of discontentment, dissatisfaction, stress and exhaustion.

If you're cynical about this spiritual, intuitive side of yourself, consider the following. Have you ever:

Listened to a piece of music that moved you or gave you goosebumps?

Watched a film that made you laugh or cry?

Witnessed a sporting triumph or human achievement that made your heart swell, brought tears to your eyes or gave you butterflies in your tummy?

Felt a natural high from being in a crowd at a football match, concert, church service or dance club?

Felt chills down your spine in the presence of a work of art, a magnificent building or a sacred place?

Witnessed such natural beauty that it took your breath away?

Shared time or conversation with another and experienced a lightness of being?

These experiences are times when your spirit has tapped into a greater spiritual energy outside of yourself, making you feel at one with the world, safe and joyous. This is the energy that nourishes your heart and soul. It is uplifting — a natural high that comes from your spirit reaching out to and connecting with the spirits of others, both past and present. It is when you feel truly at home in this world.

The Drive of Your Life has been compiled in the belief that when you tap into this spiritual side of yourself:

You know you're a great driver.

You know *where you want to go.*

You know *how to get there.*

You know *when something's wrong.*

You know *when you're lost.*

You know *you possess the compassion, love, kindness and laughter to get the maximum enjoyment and pleasure from your journey.*

Activity 2
Creating a Toolkit

☺ Now, take your notebook and list all those times and/or experiences when you've felt truly moved and a sense of belonging to the world around you.

- Collect together your memories of these times in the form of music, photographs, films, art, videos, literature, poetry, news reports – anything that helps you to evoke this feeling.

- Listen to the music, watch the films, read the books, absorb the pictures. Make a point of connecting to this energy as often as possible, and look for new ways to experience it. It's a good feeling – enjoy it, luxuriate in it. By doing this you will begin to feel more nourished, whole and complete.

Now, let's meet your support team.

Your Support Team

3

3
Your Support Team

There are two members of your support team who will always travel with you. Every time you climb into your car, they'll climb right in behind you. One of them you probably know very well; the other, you probably don't. Let's meet them both.

Your Mind

He is the part of you who *thinks*:

> *You'll never make it in that car!*

> *I don't like the look of that!*

You'll be ripped off at that garage!

I'd wait until you can afford a new car before planning to drive there!

If you don't fill up now, there might not be another chance!

You don't want to go that way, you'll hit the traffic!

There are road works ahead, you'll have to do a detour!

What if you break down? You'll never manage!

You don't want to be out in that weather!

Your Mind does all of your thinking for you. At best, he's your rational side. At worst, he's your neurotic side, the part of you that tries to control your driving style and every part of your journey. Our Mind is important though, as he can help us process information logically and rationally, thereby acting as our very own factory-fitted alarm system. Unfortunately, he can be so powerful that many of us end up constantly pulling over or even immobilised, stuck in the garage.

Your Spirit

She is the part of you who *knows*:

> *You are the best driver for your car.*

> *Where you want to go.*

> *How you can get there.*

When you need to refuel.

When you need to take a break.

When you're in real danger.

Your Spirit looks after your emotional and spiritual welfare, communicating with you through your intuition, your gut feelings, your heartfelt instincts. She's important for showing you compassion, love, kindness, laughter and forgiveness. If you listen to and trust your Spirit's advice, she can tell you what is truly right for you or what makes you unhappy or uncomfortable. Connecting to your Spirit and letting her guide your journey in this way can lead you to your destiny, your true vocation. It can also provide you with endless energy and the motivation to help you get there.

Between them, our Spirit and our Mind are our greatest support system. But many of us think too much and trust too little — we are so dominated by our Mind that we often override our Spirit, forgetting to trust what she's trying to tell us. Some of us are even frightened of our Spirit, because trusting her advice can mean taking a different route to the one our Mind thinks we should be heading along. However, we repress and ignore this side of ourselves at our peril. Learning to listen to and trust your spiritual side will help liberate you from the gridlock of shoulds and oughts, the feeling of something missing, and the need for others' permission or approval to drive.

From here on, this book will refer to our rational side as our Mind, using the masculine gender; and our instinctive, intuitive side as our Spirit, using the feminine gender. Please substitute your own names and genders for these parts of yourself, as you see fit.

Activity 3

Creating a Relaxation Ritual

Some of us may have trouble connecting to our Spirit, because we need to be totally relaxed if we are to hear our intuition or feel our gut instinct clearly and properly. If our Mind has got us all stressed and uptight, the messages sent from our Spirit will be scrambled and blocked. If this is the case, it's important for us to create a relaxation ritual.

How do you relax? What works for you? Do you ever feel truly relaxed? If you haven't got a way that works for you, here's your chance to devise one.

☺ Much of driving is ritual – before setting off we all go through the mirror-signal-manoeuvre procedure. It is much the same with relaxing. You could try using some of the following methods to create a ritual that works for you:

Light a candle or burn some incense…

Experience silence or listen to music…

Say a prayer or a mantra…

Sit down, lie down or do some stretching…

Cuddle or stroke a pet or soft toy…

Sniff something evocative such as perfume or suntan lotion…

Take a bath…

Do some deep breathing until you feel your body unwinding — breathe in to a count of seven and out to a count of eleven.

Listen to a meditation tape...

Make your own tape of you talking yourself down to a quiet, calm place...

Imagine yourself lying on a beach, chilling out by a river, relaxing in your favourite spot...

By using your senses and your imagination you will be able to stop thinking and start relaxing, thereby creating the right environment for hearing what your Spirit wants to tell you.

Activity 4

Getting to Know Your Team

It's time to get your notebook out, as we're now going to get to know these two parts of you – your Mind and your Spirit.

☺ So, thinking about these two sides of yourself, see if you can:

> *Visualise them.*

> *Draw them.*

> *Name them.*

> *Find and cut out pictures of them.*

> *Base them on people you know or on celebrities.*

☺ If you're still having trouble getting in touch with your Spirit, relax and try to imagine putting your Mind in the passenger seat of your car. Have a chat to him. What's he worrying about? Calm him down, thank him for his concern and drop him off somewhere pleasant where he can unwind for a while – by the beach, by a beautiful lake, up in the mountains. Make him comfortable and drive off.

☺ Then ask your Spirit to come and sit beside you. Ask her about a specific problem you may be experiencing. What advice has she got for you? Enjoy her presence, feel the emotions she is giving you.

☺ You may get a sudden insight or a strong gut or intuitive feeling in answer to the question you have asked your Spirit. But if this is not the case, trust her and be patient – you will get answers in the form of:

Coincidences, quirks of fate or synchronicity of events.

Bumping into someone who could help you.

Getting a helpful phone call out of the blue.

Something jumping out at you in a newspaper or magazine, or on television.

Insights and messages in the form of dreams.

So, with that under your belt, let's see how listening to your Spirit and using your intuition can help you get more enjoyment and pleasure from your journey. We'll start with your driving skills. Do you believe you're a good enough driver?

Are You A Good Enough Driver?

4

4
Are You a Good Enough Driver?

What do you need to be a good driver? Is it the make and model of your car? Do you need ABS or power-assisted steering, a powerful engine, air-conditioning or cruise control? What about a state-of-the-art entertainment system, metallic paintwork, alloy wheels or a rear spoiler? Perhaps you need plenty of money for fuel and maintenance? Or are detailed maps, helpful passengers, clear roads and good weather conditions essential?

Actually, it's none of these things. Think about it – could any of them pass your driving test for you? No. Some of them may help you out or enhance your journey, but at the end of the day, the only thing that makes you a good enough driver to pass a test is your belief in your ability to do so.

Many of us face self-doubt during some or even all parts of our journey. The aim of this section is to help you accept that you're good enough to drive wherever you choose to travel.

Activity 5

Your Licence to Drive

⊕ Take your notebook and fill in the following application form. If it helps, stick a photograph of yourself at the top of the page.

This exercise is not about self-improvement, it's about self-acceptance. When answering the questions, it's easy to let your Mind have his say at the expense of your Spirit. So, go through your Relaxation Ritual (see pp. 19–21) and ask your

Spirit for guidance. Be honest – there's nothing to be gained from lying. And above all, have fun doing it!

What do you like?
What do you dislike?

What do you enjoy?
What don't you enjoy?

What is fun for you?
What are you scared of?

What's good about you?
What's not good about you?

When do you praise yourself?
When do you criticise yourself?

What do you deserve?
What don't you deserve?

What do you want that you don't have?

Describe your ideal life.

List ten things that you enjoy doing.

☺ If you have trouble answering the above questions, you might try imagining yourself driving along a stretch of road with beautiful scenery all around you. As you journey, you stop to pick up a succession of hitchhikers who are all you at different stages of your life — child, teenager, young adult, mature adult, aging adult, and so on. Have a chat with yourself at these different stages. How are things going? What are your problems? What are your dreams? How have things changed? Using whatever methods work for you, spend time getting to know yourself and what makes you feel good.

☺ Now take your list of ten things you enjoy doing, get out your diary and schedule a time for you to do each and every one of them. Make appointments with yourself and don't break them. You'd never break a doctor's appointment, so don't cheat on yourself and your pleasure. Even if you can only spare 30 minutes a day, go out and take that walk, start that painting, visit that museum, listen to that music.

☺ Use the information in your notebook to make a list of all the positive images and beliefs you hold about yourself. Focus on these and refer back to the list during times of self-doubt.

☺ Then use the same information to list all the negative and limiting self-beliefs you have uncovered – all the reasons you think you're not really good enough to drive where you want to go.

This second list is your baggage – all the stuff banging about in your boot, distracting you and weighing you down. Let's sort it out.

The Baggage In Your Boot

5
The Baggage in Your Boot

Most of us have a certain amount of baggage, while some of us have so much we need a roof rack or small trailer to accommodate it. What's important here is that you realise that:

> Your baggage *is…*
> *experiences/feelings/states of mind.*

> Your baggage *is not…*
> *you.*

So, in this sense:

You are not sad…
you are feeling sad.

You are not a failure…
you are experiencing failure.

You are not stupid…
you are feeling stupid.

You are not lonely…
you are experiencing loneliness.

Think of your baggage as negative energy that has become trapped in the boot of your car, weighing you down and holding you back. What we're going to do now is to open the boot and release that energy. This will create room for compassionate thoughts and feelings which will help speed you on your way to getting more enjoyment from your journey.

Activity 6
Offloading Excess Baggage

To release energy, you need to be relaxed. If you're full of tension, you'll block the energy and it won't be able to escape. So, start by going through your Relaxation Ritual (see pp. 19–21).

☺   When you feel ready, take out your first piece of baggage, open it up and take a closer look:

What is it?

Relive the event or experience.

Relive the feeling in your tummy.

Ask your Spirit to help you imagine it in a different way.

Relive it again and imagine yourself feeling differently about it — happy, sad, angry, calm.

Now imagine your Spirit is giving you advice as to how you can make it better. Or imagine you're advising your best friend, child or loved one — how would you make them feel better about it?

Let your Spirit show you compassion, kindness, laughter and hope.

Above all, forgive yourself and all those involved — bless them and move on.

☻ If this is difficult, here are some alternative methods you could try:

> Get some photographs of the people who were involved in the event or experience, and imagine talking it through with them.

> Imagine yourself driving along a beautiful road. Pick up the people who were involved as hitchhikers, have a chat, sort it out and drop them off.

> Get a mirror and talk yourself through it.

> Ask a friend to talk it through with you.

> Write a letter to a friend about it.

> Pretend it was a friend who wrote the letter, and counsel her through it – be your own best friend.

☺ When you feel you've changed your feelings about the event, experience or people involved, do something symbolic:

Plant a seed…

Clear out a cupboard…

Throw something away…

Burn something…

Rip the letter up or burn it…

Have a bath or a shower…

Do something physical like going for a walk, jogging, cycling, dancing…

⊕ The way you choose to release this negative energy is not important. What counts is asking your Spirit to show you compassion, kindness, forgiveness and hope while you're doing it. As you sort through your baggage in this way, you should begin to feel lighter and more open to the enjoyment and pleasure your journey can offer you.

⊕ To help you overcome any persistent self-doubt, make a set of cards – like playing cards – but instead of writing on numbers, write positive thoughts about yourself. To help you, refer back to the lists you made in Activity 5, reversing all the negative and limiting self-beliefs you may hold about yourself. Use your Spirit to show yourself the love and compassion to do this. For example:

Excess Baggage
Helpful Baggage

I am stupid.
I have all the intelligence I need.

I am fat.
I am getting slimmer and healthier each day.

I am sad.
I can comfort myself and feel better.

I'm not good enough.
I accept and love myself for who I am.

I am guilty.
I do not judge myself by others' values.

I am a victim.

I am in control of my journey and its direction.

Okay, so maybe now you're starting to get excited about your potential and your journey again, but what about your driving companions? Let's look at ways of getting the maximum enjoyment and support from them.

Your Driving Companions

6

Your Driving Companions

When it comes to carrying passengers, what sort of driver are you? Do you agree to take someone to the shops even if it's out of your way and you haven't really got enough fuel? Or do you take no notice of your passengers' comfort and enjoyment of the ride? Do you resent having passengers? Do they confuse you, annoy you, make you feel guilty for not taking their chosen route?

Perhaps you are happier as a passenger, letting someone else dictate your journey? Or are you a back-seat driver, constantly worrying that your chauffeur isn't taking the best roads or that the car will run out of fuel? Perhaps you avoid asking to be taken to your exact destination, agreeing instead to travel somewhere even though you know it's not where you want to go?

It would be wonderful to fill our cars with fun, supportive and undemanding passengers, who can even do minor repair work when we break down. Or to be a passenger in a comfortable, warm car, driven by someone whose sole aim is to please us and take us exactly where we want to go. But the truth is that although at times our journey may be like this, at other times it won't. Let's look at dealing with those times.

Chauffeuring

We all have to act as a chauffeur from time to time. Often it means taking a detour from our chosen route and consuming fuel we could have used on ourselves. Yet doing everything alone can be exhausting, draining and isolating.

Passengers can be fantastic and can enhance our enjoyment of the journey.

What's important is to chauffeur others in the right spirit, from a place of love and compassion, and not from a place of expectation. If you drive someone around with the unspoken expectation that they will do the same for you, or value or love you more, then you will often end up disappointed, feeling like a victim and acting like a martyr. This behaviour is neither attractive nor helpful – when someone takes on the cloak of martyrdom, nobody wins.

Expectations can so often ruin things, leading us to feel dependent on our passengers or seeking to control them. Under these circumstances, enjoyment of our companions plays second fiddle to games of power and manipulation. If you cannot chauffeur someone without having expectations of what they'll do for you, then it's best to let them know.

Spell it out, so it's a fair trade-off — I'll take you to the supermarket on Thursdays, if you check my oil; or I'll drop you at the library, if you wash the car. Remember, if you expect something back, communicate it and be specific about it.

Any change can be difficult. If you've always taken someone to the supermarket and suddenly you decide not to, or start asking for things in return, it is natural for the person concerned to feel confused, upset, angry or worried. This doesn't have to be a problem. Either explain where you're going and that you can no longer make the necessary detour for them; or better still, build them into a support network. As before, explain where you want to get to yourself and offer to carry on helping the person out, if they're prepared to do the same for you.

Being a Passenger

Being a passenger is unavoidable. Sometimes our car breaks down, runs out of fuel, or needs a service. This can either be fun, adventurous and a chance to experience a different route, or it can be frustrating and deeply irritating to have to detour from our chosen road and rely on others. But there are ways to maximise the rewards and enjoyment of these times.

Firstly, we can accept that for this part of our journey we are a passenger, and sit back and enjoy the ride. If this doesn't feel comfortable for you, avoid trying to impose your driving style or chosen route on your chauffeur, either by unspoken, manipulative behaviour or by outright demands. Imagine how this would make you feel if you were driving, and the potential for resentment and anger it could cause. In this situation, again think about what you could do to help both your chauffeur and yourself.

Bypassing the Guilty Ring Road

This can all be so good, but there are a couple of feelings that may block your path – guilt, and not being honest about what you want. Guilt stems from being intimidated by other people's values at the expense of your own. It is fear of others' disapproval. To overcome this, you must accept and approve of yourself and your values above all others.

Similarly, if you aren't honest about what you feel and what you want, you're rejecting yourself in favour of what you think someone else wants to hear. But *you* count! What *you* think and feel matters! We all have a deep need to feel connected as though we belong. But not being honest or true to ourselves, in the hope that others will like or love us more, won't bring us the sense of belonging, the peace, satisfaction and enjoyment of our journey we deserve. In fact, this behaviour is likely to result in our relationships becoming a source of stress, as we try to control others or end up feeling dependent upon them.

Activity 7

Learning to Indicate

☺ Taking out your notebook, devise ways that both you and your driving companions can help one another get the most from your respective journeys.

The important thing is to communicate, being both honest and specific about needs and desires, and how they can be met. Don't just offer to amuse the kids in the back of the car, for instance – offer to do it between 2.30 and 4pm.

Above all, drive with compassion and love, and enjoy those whose journeys you share!

Activity 8

Turning off the Guilty Highway

☺   If feelings of guilt crop up for you, get out your notebook. Go through your Relaxation Ritual (pp.19–21), then ask your Spirit for guidance and yourself these questions:

> *Why do I make it difficult for people to help me?*

> *Why do I reject offers of help?*

> *Why do I pretend I want something, or want to do something, when I don't?*

> *Why do I pretend I don't want something, or don't want to do something, when I do?*

Why do I say no when I want to say yes?

Why do I say yes when I want to say no?

Why do I judge myself by other people's values?

Why don't I judge myself by what's acceptable to me?

Imagine a scenario involving your child or your best friend, in which they weren't being honest, or were fearful of trying something they really wanted to do, or scared of fulfilling their beauty, success or intelligence. What advice would you offer them? Surely you would encourage them to try to fulfil their potential, to make the most of what they have to offer, to make their journey as enjoyable and satisfying as possible. Ask your Spirit for advice and guidance, and show this love, encouragement and compassion to yourself.

☺ Remember, the best way for us to feel a true sense of belonging to the world around us comes from our Spirits tapping into a spiritual energy that's bigger than our own. If this is an issue for you, seek solace in your toolkit of memories of times when you felt this sense of belonging, as you did back in Activity 2 (see pp.10–11).

Working with your Spirit in this way, and acting as your own best friend, frees you up to enjoy your travelling companions. It means that you've no need to feel dependent on them or controlling of them.

We're now going to take a closer look at uncomfortable feelings and how to deal with them, so they don't distract us from the pleasure we could be getting from our journey.

Dealing With Road Rage

7

Dealing with Road Rage

When someone cuts you up, do you tremble in terror and pull over, or do you press your foot firmly on the accelerator and give chase? Are you someone who revs up at the lights determined to be first off the starting grid, or have you been known to drive deliberately slowly to annoy the person behind you? Road rage and many other emotions – even much happier ones, such as joy and excitement – can be scary for some of us. We worry about:

Being overwhelmed by the emotions.

Expressing them, in case they conflict with our self-image.

Getting stuck in them, instead of simply experiencing them.

In the case of happy feelings, that we don't deserve them or they won't last.

In fact, many of us can be so worried about letting ourselves feel emotions that we repress them by distracting ourselves with food, drink or drugs. Or we avoid them by acting helpless and playing the victim/martyr game.

But emotions are neither good nor bad. They are simply energies inside of us, often felt in our tummies. It's only when we ignore or repress these energies that they can get stuck, or build up to such an intensity that they explode out of us like an erupting volcano. The trick is to find ways of expressing energy that feel comfortable for you.

Some of the best ways to transform and/or conduct energy include doing some form of physical activity, having a good cry, submerging yourself in water, or listening to music. So:

If you feel angry…
you could hit a cushion, go for a walk, dance, jog, cycle, shake the feeling away, play loud music, cry…

If you feel happy…
you could dance, sing, phone a friend…

If you feel stressed…
you could practise a relaxation technique, take a bath, massage yourself with body lotion…

If you feel sad…
you could cry, write down how you feel, talk to a loved one, take a bath…

It is worth mentioning here that depression is not a feeling, it's an action – the action of depressing our feelings. In mild cases, we cease to feel anything very strongly, whether good or bad. If you tend to depress your feelings, you can learn to identify and express them by practising the following activity. However, in severe cases of depression you may need to call up the rescue services to help you back on the road to recovery (see Major Accidents and Breakdowns, page 109).

Activity 9

Express Yourself

☺ Using your notebook, list the feelings you have difficulty expressing. Try to think of what you could do to experience and move this energy through you in a way that feels comfortable. Again, ask your Spirit to help you do this from a place of love and compassion.

59

☺ If you have trouble actually identifying your feelings, go through your Relaxation Ritual (pp.19–20), putting your Mind to bed and asking your Spirit for guidance. Concentrate on what you're feeling in your tummy:

What colour is the feeling?

What animal?

Does it remind you of anyone you know?

Once you've identified it and let yourself feel it, try transforming it. Change the colour, morph the animal or person. Or just think of the feeling as energy or air that you are letting flow through you, to be replaced by something more comfortable:

From fear…
to excitement

From sad…
to hopeful

From stress…
to comfort

From anger…
to calm

One of the most common distractions from uncomfortable feelings involves fuel consumption – too much or too little. Let's take a closer look.

Mastering Fuel Consumption

8

Mastering Fuel Consumption

Would you put petrol in a diesel car? Put diesel in a petrol car? Put too little fuel in for the length of your journey? Put more fuel in your tank than it can hold? No. Yet many of us try to journey on tanks of excess food and alcohol, or fill up with fuel that's full of salt or chemicals such as artificial sweeteners and preservatives. Is it any wonder that we often struggle to enjoy our travels, feel too exhausted to move, or don't even know where we're heading?

Fuel is the one thing we cannot live without. It is vital, our very life force – without it we could not journey at all. That's why every car has a fuel gauge which warns us when we're running low on fuel. Some gauges may even make a beeping noise as the tank nears empty. Well, guess what? Every driver has one of these devices, too.

Do you realise that fuel is something you need never have to worry about again? We've all got an inbuilt fuel gauge. So, while you concentrate on enjoying your journey, your tummy will rumble for you when you need to refuel. It will even tell you when you're satisfied – if you listen to it. You don't even have to worry about the type of fuel you need. Your body knows what it wants – fuel that can quickly and easily be converted into energy. This includes:

Fresh foods, vegetables, fruit, eggs

Pure water or juice

Anything unprocessed, such as grains, cereals, nuts, rice

Lean meat and fish that have been reared naturally

It's easy! You get on with your journey, eating the above foodstuffs when you're hungry and stopping when you're satisfied. You continue on your way until your tummy tells you it's time to find another garage.

But some of us have made our lives far more complicated than this. Refuelling has nothing to do with having an empty tank. Instead, it's about:

> *Distracting ourselves from road rage, or other uncomfortable emotions or situations.*

> *Comforting ourselves when we're stuck in traffic, have broken down, feel lost…*

Yet, because this sort of eating is not about hunger, we never feel satisfied. We might eat a packet of biscuits, a tub of ice cream, a multipack of crisps, or even a seven-course meal.

And although physically we may feel unbearably bloated, we still do not feel emotionally full and satisfied. So:

> *If we are angry and eat or binge to distract ourselves, even once we've finally managed to stop, all we've done is to stuff the anger down. The anger is still there, and it's the reason why, however much we've eaten, we still aren't satisfied.*

> *If we are in need of comfort, and again we use fuel to soothe us, we can eat until the cows come home without ever having that need for comfort satisfied.*

Consequently, after each episode of this type of behaviour, we are not only left with the emotion we've tried to stuff down our throats but also with a negative view of ourselves:

Why did I do that?

Why couldn't I stop?

Some of us misuse fuel in a different way. Instead of stuffing the emotion down, we try to starve it out of ourselves. But again, this behaviour is just a distraction from dealing with the real cause of the problem – not being comfortable with our feelings, and not knowing how to experience and express them in a way that is acceptable to us.

Acitivity 10

Fuel Tank Management

- So, what to do? Look back over the Dealing with Road Rage chapter again (pp.55–61), and learn how to recognise, express and enjoy your feelings and emotions. Stop stuffing them down or starving them out. Own them, be proud of them – they're what makes us human and what makes you, you!

- Let yourself get physically hungry. Once you are, ask your body what it wants to eat – crunchy, stodgy, smooth, lumpy, cold, hot, and so on. Try to satisfy it with the best possible fuel you have available. Your body knows what it wants, and rarely does this involve fuel that's full of salt or chemicals. The more you do this, the better your communication with your body will get.

- Stop eating when you feel satisfied and *not* when you feel full. This can take some practice, but again, the more you do it, the easier it becomes. Concentrate on what you eat, deriving the maximum pleasure and satisfaction from it. Eat slowly, and listen to your body telling you when you've had enough.

The next time you eat something when you're not physically hungry, or force yourself not to eat something when you are physically hungry, work out why you behaved like that. Was it:

To be polite?

Because you felt bored?

Because you felt stressed?

Because you needed to be comforted?

Because you felt angry?

Because you were worried you might miss out on something?

Because you wanted to feel in control?

Write down in your notebook how else you could have satisfied these feelings, and next time try to do things differently. Remember to do this with the help of your Spirit, with love, compassion and forgiveness.

🙂 Never diet. In the long run diets don't work, because all they do is keep your eyes on the fuel gauge – all your energy is spent worrying about refuelling and hanging around petrol stations. Don't waste your journey or distract yourself from enjoying it by worrying about fuel. Raise your eyes, get out there on the open road, and start enjoying yourself!

Now, let's take a look at what else we can do to keep ourselves performing at our optimum level for pleasure and enjoyment.

9
Recharging Your Battery

To keep our cars ticking over and roadworthy, we need to keep the battery charged — and the easiest way to do this is to use it. This doesn't have to mean a daily 25-mile workout, putting it through all its paces. This can be too disruptive, distract us from our journey and, once the initial enthusiasm has worn off, actually put us off going out altogether. Just slightly raising activity levels as part of our daily routine is all it takes. So, you might want to consider some of the following:

> *Walk or cycle to school/town/work — or at least part of the way.*

Play outdoor games with the children.

Walk the dog.

Take up gardening.

Use the stairs, not the lift.

Do some stretching and/or toning exercises while watching TV.

Make a dance tape of your favourite records, then get up and get moving!

Take part in a sport you enjoy.

For most of us, this type of increased activity level will be perfectly adequate for keeping our batteries charged. Yet, physical activity is one of the greatest shifters of energy we have. It is worth cultivating as one of the fastest routes to coping with difficult feelings, offloading baggage, and feeling good about ourselves and our journey. So do try to incorporate more than just the necessary into your schedule. If the word 'exercise' is a turnoff, think of yourself as having a 'well-being session'.

Activity 11

Making Physical Exercise a Habit

☺ None of the activities suggested above needs to be too disruptive. Think about your daily routine and write down in your notebook all the ways in which you could be more active.

☺ When it comes to more demanding physical exercise, there are now so many available options that you're bound to find something to suit and motivate you personally. Start by considering the following:

Do you prefer to exercise alone or with others?

Do you prefer to be outside or indoors?

Do you want to improve your ability, compete or simply enjoy yourself?

Do you prefer to have an instructor and the discipline of a set class, or would you rather work out at home?

Do you feel like doing something calming, or do you want to get hot and sweaty?

Again, the trick is to learn to listen to our bodies telling us what they need. These needs will often change, so don't get stuck in a rut. Instead of staying with a single chosen activity, come up with a repertoire of different ones to suit you and your moods. Here are some suggestions:

Ballet, salsa, ballroom, disco, line dancing...

Pilates, yoga, martial arts...

Swimming, jogging, cycling, walking, horse riding...

Gymnastics, aerobics, exercise classes, trampolining...

Tennis, badminton, squash...

Netball, volleyball, basketball...

Football, rugby, cricket, hockey…

Ice-skating, roller-blading, skateboarding, skiing…

Climbing, abseiling, potholing…

List all the things you might fancy and try one each week until you find one or several activities you really enjoy. Build these into your weekly schedule until you are benefitting from three-to-four sessions a week.

Switching off Your Engine

If your car starts making a knocking noise or keeps petering out, do you ignore it and continue on your way? Probably not. You pull over and try to find out what's causing the problem. Or maybe you get someone to help you find out what's wrong. Whatever the case, you investigate it and try to get it fixed.

Yet, many of us try to keep going when we feel stressed, exhausted, discontented, angry or bored. Taking time out for short breaks is vital. There are times when we all need to pull over and switch off the engine, either to work out what the problem is, or simply to rest and replenish ourselves.

Again, think of yourself as a container of energy. If you don't re-inflate, replenish and refill yourself with what you need, your journey won't be as much fun as it could be, and you'll end up feeling deflated and exhausted.

Activity 12

Losing Your Mind

⚙ Using your Relaxation Ritual every day is important. You need to turn off your Mind and connect to your Spirit to see what's going on with you. Do you just need a break? Is there something you need to resolve? What can you do to improve the situation?

☺ Making time for hobbies and interests is another important way to relax and switch off your Mind. Commit to nurturing the ones you enjoy, or take up something new. Anything that absorbs you, and lets you lose yourself in it, will do you the power of good. For ideas look back at Activity 5 (see pp.27–31), and the list you made of things you enjoy. Or you could consider:

Painting, drawing, sculpting…

Sewing, knitting, cross-stitch…

Jigsaws, model making…

Decorating, gardening…

Visiting art galleries/museums/churches…

Creative writing, watching films, reading…

Collecting things, studying…

Sport or some other sort of physical activity…

Voluntary work for an organisation you feel passionate about.

Time with friends or family…

Making music or learning to play a musical instrument.

One final point for those of you who think you haven't got time for your interests. Do you really think that racing around burning up fuel, jumping in and out of the car, and not really knowing where you're going, is helping you to enjoy your journey? Or is this simply distracting you from it?

The Weekly Car Wash

As already mentioned, water can be a great shifter of negative energy, so use it to really pamper yourself. Maybe you give your car a wash, wax and polish once a week. Try to set aside similar time for yourself, and really feel yourself caring for your body. Pride in your appearance is important. It is not vanity.

Activity 13

Washing, Waxing and Polishing

- Put aside some time each week to pamper yourself. Do this pampering consciously. Let the water relax you and the cleansing invigorate you. Soothe yourself by massaging in creams and lotions.

- If you find such pampering difficult, imagine you are helping your child or a friend to get ready to go out. Spend the time, care and attention that you'd give to them on yourself.

So, now you're all dressed up, let's see where you want to go!

Route Planning

CAUTION NEW ROAD AHEAD

Route Planning

✦ ✦ ✦ ✦

The Drive of Your Life doesn't have to be about changing your life or direction. Instead it is about using your Spirit, intuition, love, compassion and laughter to enjoy yourself on your journey. Yet there will be times when you may wish to change direction, or to enhance one or other areas of your life. This chapter will help you to enjoy making those changes.

So, let's look at where you want to go and what might be stopping you from getting there. Scared you won't make it? Scared you will? For some of us, it can seem so much easier to travel along well-worn paths, because:

We know the way.

We know how to negotiate every twist and turn in the road.

We know where we'll end up — even if it's not where we want to be, it's familiar and safe.

Our passengers expect us to take that route.

Still, at least those people are out there, travelling. There are others of us who decide that before we set off, we'll just wait until:

The road is completely clear.

The weather conditions are perfect.

We can be sure there will be no roadworks or detours.

Our car has been serviced and is in tiptop condition.

We've sorted out our fuel problems.

The passengers we want are available for the ride.

But even if you've avoided these pitfalls, how do you know where you want to go? And how do you find a map to take you there? Driving in the right Spirit, using your intuition, will lead you to your destiny. It will also mobilise endless magic, energy and motivation to support you.

Activity 14

Your Dream Destination

⊕ Using your Relaxation Ritual (see pp.19–21), put your
Mind to bed and ask your Spirit to help you out with
this one. When you're ready:

> *Take an area of your life you would like either to
> enhance or to change direction.*

> *Asking your Spirit for advice, use your imagination
> simply to fantasise – or daydream, if you like –
> about this area of your life.*

> *In an ideal world, what would this area of your life
> be like?*

> *What would you be doing?*

Who are you with?

Where are you?

How would you be behaving?

How would others be reacting to you?

Once you've really indulged yourself, and let your imagination run wild, bring yourself back to reality.

   If you have problems doing the above, focus on what you enjoy doing now, or think back to what you used to enjoy doing as a child, teenager or young adult. Are there any clues? What do you need to be doing to feel comfortable and satisfied?

To be alone…
or to be with others?

To be outside…
or to be indoors?

To travel…
or to be at home?

To be physically active…
or to be more sedentary?

To be with people…
or to be with animals?

To teach…
or to learn?

To feel free...
or to have discipline?

To perform...
or to work backstage?

To support others...
or to be supported by others?

☺ Take out your notebook and write down your ideal scenario. Or you might like to draw it, or use scrap art or press cuttings to portray it. Or maybe you would prefer to write a letter either to yourself or a friend, explaining all about your new life. This is the information you need to decide your destination and map your route for getting there. Have fun doing this, and make it as fabulous as possible.

⊕ Now awaken your Mind and ask him for his input. He may come up with all sorts of reasons why it can't be done, but just thank him and write them down. These reasons and problems will act as stepping stones to your chosen destination. Any limiting self-beliefs or negative thoughts that come up can be worked on as excess baggage, as we did in Activity 6 (see pp.36–42).

⊕ Then, taking each perceived problem one at a time, brainstorm as many solutions as you can come up with, however ridiculous these may at first appear. You might prefer to do your brainstorming alone or with a group of friends. Remember that people like to help and solve problems – a team of you will generate a whole host of possibilities, contacts and ideas to get you started on your journey.

The difference between hoping and wishing for something, and making it happen, is your *intent*. You have to decide and believe that it *is* what you want, that it *is* what you were born to do. Then the energy and power behind your decision and belief will move mountains. In fact, the only obstacle to attaining any goal is the belief that you can't do it. Change your beliefs and you can change your Mind. When this happens, you'll find that your Mind will start to help you achieve your goals.

Mapping Your Journey

Mapping Your Journey

✳✳✳✳

Knowing your destination is the key to mapping the route. So once you know where you want to get to, you may need to start researching what opportunities and/or classes are available locally, and whether you need any particular qualifications. It may help to set up a network of people who can offer help or advice that relates specifically to your goal – people who are already doing what you hope to do, for instance. Or you could link up with others who are pursuing different destinations, and form a support group so that you can help one another when the going gets tough.

A few words of caution here: avoid getting caught at the traffic lights of perfection, and don't get frustrated if you get stuck behind slow-moving vehicles. Perfection and impatience will conspire to make your journey more stressful and less pleasurable. Trust that everything is evolving in the right way and at the right pace for you. As long as you stay focused on your belief and desire to reach your destination, you will get there.

The important thing is to enjoy the journey. You have only one journey, so don't waste it. If you don't like your current scenery, you can change it!

Activity 15

Changing Direction

☺ Once you've decided where you want to go, and you really believe you can get there, take all the information you've uncovered with the help of your Spirit and your Mind, and use it to work out a goal plan. Think about where you want to be, and what you

97

want to achieve, over the next weeks, months and years. So, for example, if your heart's desire is to be an actor, your goal plan might look something like this:

Becoming an Actor
Time frame

Research local courses/drama societies
1 week

Join course/society
1 month

Subscribe to relevant trade magazines
3 months

Win role in local production or stage own
production
1 year

Audition for bigger roles
2 years

Obtain Equity card
3 years

Take part in major production
5 years

12
Making Decisions

12
Making Decisions

Sometimes you hit a crossroads or fork in the road and you are paralysed by indecision. You can drive yourself mad trying to work out which route leads to eternal peace and enlightenment, and which leads to gridlock and road rage. There is a simple way out, though – you just have to accept that neither is better or worse, the roads are simply different. Whichever one you take, there will be opportunities to learn and obstacles to overcome.

Once you've decided which way to turn, you need to give up all expectations of what that road may offer you. If not, you'll miss opportunities and encounter disappointments when things aren't how you've imagined them. Keep your eyes open and concentrate – drive with due care and attention. That way you'll be open to opportunities you might have otherwise overlooked.

Activity 16

Turning Left or Right?

☺ When making a decision, it helps to do your homework. Get your Mind on the job and have him research all the rational data for each route. Then let your Spirit kick in – relax and ask her advice. A quick way of doing this is to toss a coin. Before it lands, your gut instinct will usually tell you which way up you want it to fall.

☺ New roads can feel strange. If when you start out on yours, you immediately have the urge to turn back, pull over for a while. Using your Relaxation Ritual (see pp.19–21), ask your Spirit what's bothering you, and what you can do in order to find this new, uncharted territory interesting, rewarding and exciting.

Overcoming Obstacles

13

ON
TOW

#

Overcoming Obstacles

✷ ✷ ✷ ✷

Whichever way you journey, you will encounter problems. The trick is to create value from them, so you learn something, grow stronger, and increase in confidence. It's a nuisance if you get a flat tyre – it slows you down and may cost you money. On the positive side, however, the person who comes to your aid could end up as a good friend or even become the love of your life. You might learn how to mend the flat tyre. You might miss being involved in an accident further up the road. Or you might even get to a garage where they're short-staffed and end up with a new job.

The thing is to keep your eyes open as to how you can get something positive from the situation, however dire.

Worrying about problems is not a solution – worrying is the alarm. Acting to resolve them is what counts.

Activity 17
Stop Worrying and Start Acting

When you hit a problem ask yourself:

What is the worst-case scenario here?

What is the ideal scenario?

Follow this up by researching your options or choices – you always have a choice, even if it's to do nothing. Back this up by:

Asking your Spirit for guidance.

Deciding what action to take.

Taking action.

Parking your worries.

Starting to trust.

Even if it's not appropriate to act immediately, just deciding what to do and when to do it will help to alleviate your worries.

This can all be very helpful, but sometimes we need to call in the experts. Let's look now at who can help.

Major Accidents And Breakdowns 14

14

Major Accidents and Breakdowns

Major accidents and breakdowns can be a serious warning that something is wrong, and falling ill or suffering misfortune is sometimes a cry for help. Often you can repair and cure yourself by:

Taking time out to relax.

Eating and drinking the best possible foods to enable your body to work properly.

Recharging your battery with regular moderate activity.

Giving your Mind the slip and getting absorbed in hobbies and interests.

Self-help techniques such as those described here and, in more detail, in the vast library of other books now available on the subject.

Calling on your support team of people willing to help each other out.

Taking a short break, holiday, retreat…

Doing something outside of your normal environment – visiting a new place, catching up with an old friend, taking up a new activity or hobby…

But sometimes we need help. This may just be talking things over with a loved one or a friend we trust. But certain issues can go deeper. For example, if you are unable to cope with depression, or an eating, drinking or drug problem, you will need professional help. In such cases, there are two main rescue services you can call upon:

> *Conventional medicine, which would start with a visit to your GP and may involve medication and/or counselling or other psychiatric help.*

> *Complementary medicine, which could involve the services of an aromatherapist, acupuncturist, homeopath, naturopath, nutritionist, craniosacral therapist, herbalist, and so on.*

Some GPs may also be happy to discuss complementary medicine with you, and even to recommend practitioners. If this is not the case, do research the qualifications and credibility of complementary practitioners, as currently they do not need a licence to practise. A good port of call is the society or governing body of the discipline you're interested in, which should be able to help out with accredited practitioners in your area. Alternatively, word of mouth recommendations can also be an important factor when making your choice.

Above all else, do not be afraid to ask for help. Nobody deserves to endure a broken Spirit and a miserable journey. Reach out, and someone, somewhere will come to your aid – but you do need to make that first move.

Activity 18

Developing a First Aid Kit

☺ Use your notebook to collect and store information, articles, cuttings and advertisements about people, products and services designed to help you feel better. Build up a library of information and ideas covering various physical, emotional and mental health topics that could be of help to you and others in the future.

Servicing And MOTs

15
Servicing and MOTs

To give yourself the best chance of getting the maximum pleasure and enjoyment from your journey, here's a checklist of things that can help:

> *Connecting regularly to a spiritual, uplifting energy bigger than yourself.*
>
> *Listening to and taking directions from your Spirit, and treating yourself and others with compassion, kindness and forgiveness.*
>
> *Carrying a positive self-image and a strong self-belief.*

Regularly offloading your excess baggage.

Nurturing your driving companions as a source of joy and support.

Honouring your feelings.

Consuming appropriate quantities of high-performance fuel.

Keeping your battery charged by doing moderate physical activity.

Taking regular breaks for relaxing, developing your interests, and losing your Mind.

Physically pampering yourself.

Devising, planning and driving along a route in life that brings you personal satisfaction and joy.

Activity 19

Keeping a Service Manual

☺ Take out your notebook and pinpoint a time every month to give yourself a mini-service. Consider the above suggestions and make sure you are looking after yourself in the best possible way.

☺ Set dates at six-monthly intervals for a full MOT – you could do this with a friend if you think it might be more fun. Use this time to assess how you're doing with respect to your goals. Have your goals changed? But more importantly, are you enjoying the journey towards them? If you're not, reassess. And remember to trust that everything is coming to you at a pace or time that is right for you. Being impatient is just another way of condemning yourself to a stressful ride.

You can also use your MOT time to look at the overall balance in different areas of your life. There will always be times when some areas demand more of your attention than others, but are there some you are neglecting? If one area has met a roadblock or suffered a breakdown, can you find comfort and solace from another?

These sessions can help you redefine or clarify your goals for the following six months, when you can check in again and repeat the process. Remember, the key is to drive in the right Spirit, enjoy your journey, and get out of it what is right and comfortable for you.

Keeping On Track

16
Keeping on Track

⊕   You're lost if you feel:

Confused   Stressed

Dissatisfied   Scared

Discontented   Isolated

Exhausted

☺ You're on track if you feel:

Compassionate   *Adventurous*

Joyful   *Trusting*

Creative   *Excited*

Forgiving   *Safe*

Kind

It has been the aim of this book to give you some techniques and ideas to help you connect with and listen to your Spirit. You have all you need to get the maximum amount of enjoyment from your journey — don't waste it being busy and feeling exhausted, and don't distract yourself by worrying about minor repairs and fuel consumption. By learning to put your Spirit in the driving seat, you will come to love your journey and to experience the sheer joy and deep satisfaction that driving can bring!

NOTES

NOTES

NOTES

★★★★

We hope you enjoyed this Hay House book.
If you would like to receive a free catalogue featuring additional
Hay House books and products, or if you would like information
about the Hay Foundation, please contact:

Hay House UK Ltd

Unit 62, Canalot Studios • 222 Kensal Rd • London W10 5BN
Tel: (44) 20-8962-1230; Fax: (44) 20-8962-1239
www.hayhouse.co.uk

Published and distributed in the United States of America by:
Hay House, Inc. • PO Box 5100 • Carlsbad, CA 92018-5100
Tel: (1) 760-431-7695 or (800) 654-5126;
Fax: (1) 760-431-6948 or (800) 650-5115
www.hayhouse.com

Published and distributed in Australia by:
Hay House Australia Ltd • 18/36 Ralph St • Alexandria NSW 2015
Tel: (61) 2-9669-4299 • Fax: (61) 2-9669-4144
www.hayhouse.com.au

Published and distributed in the Republic of South Africa by:
Hay House SA (Pty) Ltd • PO Box 990 • Witkoppen 2068
Tel/Fax: (27) 11-706-6612 • orders@psdprom.co.za

Distributed in Canada by:
Raincoast • 9050 Shaughnessy St • Vancouver, BC V6P 6E5
Tel: (1) 604 323 7100 • Fax: (1) 604 323 2600

Sign up via the Hay House UK website to receive the Hay House
online newsletter and stay informed about what's going on with
your favourite authors. You'll receive bimonthly announcements
about discounts and offers, special events, product highlights,
free excerpts, giveaways, and more!
www.hayhouse.co.uk